STAR WARS

THE CLONE WARS

THE STARCRUSHER TRAP

SCRIPT **MIKE W. BARR**   ART **THE FILLBACH BROTHERS**

COLORS **RAYMUND LEE**   LETTERING **MICHAEL HEISLER**

COVER ART **THE FILLBACH BROTHERS WITH DAN JACKSON**

DARK HORSE BOOKS®

THE RISE OF THE EMPIRE
1000–0 YEARS BEFORE *STAR WARS: A NEW HOPE*

The events in these stories take place approximately twenty-two years before the Battle of Yavin.

After the seeming final defeat of the Sith, the Republic enters a state of complacency. In the waning years of the Republic, the Senate is rife with corruption, and the ambitious Senator Palpatine has himself elected Supreme Chancellor. This is the era of the prequel trilogy.

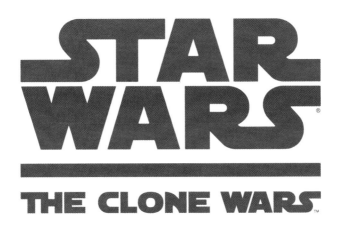

STAR WARS®

THE CLONE WARS™

THE STARCRUSHER TRAP

DESIGNER **AIMEE DANIELSON-GERMANY**

ASSISTANT EDITOR **FREDDYE LINS**

EDITOR **RANDY STRADLEY**

PUBLISHER **MIKE RICHARDSON**

Special thanks to Jann Moorhead, David Anderman, Troy Alders, Leland Chee, Sue Rostoni, and Carol Roeder at Lucas Licensing.

Published by Dark Horse Books, a division of Dark Horse Comics, Inc.
10956 SE Main Street, Milwaukie, OR 97222

DarkHorse.com | StarWars.com

To find a comics shop in your area, call the Comic Shop Locator Service toll-free at 1.888.266.4226
First edition: July 2011 | ISBN 978-1-59582-714-2

10 9 8 7 6 5 4 3 2 1
PRINTED AT SOLISCO PRINTERS, LTD., SCOTT, QC, CANADA

Library of Congress Cataloging-in-Publication Data

Barr, Mike W.

The starcrusher trap / script, Mike Barr ; art, the Fillbach Brothers ; colors, Raymund Lee ; lettering, Michael Heisler ; cover art, the Fillbach Brothers with Dan Jackson.

p. cm.

At head of title: Star wars. The clone wars.

ISBN 978-1-59582-714-2

1. Graphic novels. I. Fillbach, Shawn. II. Fillbach, Matthew. III. Jackson, Dan. IV. Title. V. Title: Star crusher trap.

PZ7.7.B366St 2011

741.5'973--dc22

2011001988

STAR WARS: THE CLONE WARS—THE STARCRUSHER TRAP

ON AN ASTEROID DEEP INSIDE ENEMY SPACE SITS A MUNITIONS FACTORY, PRODUCING WEAPONS OF WAR FOR THE SEPARATIST MOVEMENT.

PROTECTED AGAINST ALL ASSAULTS BY A FORCE FIELD, THE FACTORY HAS PROVEN TO BE INVULNERABLE TO ALL STARSHIP ATTACKS.

BUT TWO JEDI KNIGHTS MAY BE MORE FORMIDABLE THAN A FLEET OF STARSHIPS.

MASTER KENOBI, I THINK I FORGOT THE EXPLOSIVES!

WHAT?

9

ALL THREE SHIPS DESTROYED, ADMIRAL KIRST.

GOOD.

WIDE-ANGLE SPREAD. TARGET ANY ESCAPE PODS AND FIRE.

SHOULDN'T THE TASK FORCE HAVE ATTACKED BY NOW?

I WOULD HAVE THOUGHT SO. HAVE YOU CALLED FOR OUR EXTRACTION?

ON IT NOW, MASTER.

AND HERE WE ARE.

GET ABOARD QUICKLY. I DON'T LIKE THIS!

YOU CALLED FOR A TAXI?

GET US OUT OF HERE, MASTER SOMTAY-- SOMETHING'S GONE WRONG!

ARE YOU CERTAIN, MASTER KENOBI? I'VE HEARD NO REPORTS FROM THE TASK FORCE!

THAT MAY *BE* THE PROBLEM!

WHERE'D ALL THIS *WRECKAGE* COME FROM?

I'M AFRAID I *KNOW*, JYL...

...AND I THINK *THAT'S* THE REASON!

WOW...!

WELL, ARE YOU JUST GOING TO FLY *INTO* IT?

IT'S TOO LATE TO *AVOID* IT, MASTER...

...AND THOUGH THE STARCRUSHER PERFORMED ADMIRABLY, LORD SIDIOUS, HAD THE JEDI BEEN ANY EARLIER, THE FACTORY WOULD HAVE BEEN DESTROYED.

VERY WELL, COUNT DOOKU. I SHALL BE IN TOUCH.

THE JEDI. ALWAYS THE CURSED JEDI. IF HIS PLAN IS TO ACHIEVE FRUITION, THEY MUST BE ELIMINATED.

BUT HOW...?

THE SCOWL OF DARTH SIDIOUS IS THOUGHT TO BE A FEARSOME SIGHT...

OF COURSE.

...UNTIL ONE SEES HIS SMILE.

YES, VERY GRAVE THE THREAT OF THIS NEW WEAPON IS. TAKE IMMEDIATE ACTION WE MUST.

TO DESTROY THIS *"STARCRUSHER,"* A SMALL ASSAULT TEAM MOST EFFECTIVE WILL BE.

I WILL LEAD THE TEAM, MASTER YODA.

APPRECIATED YOUR SKILLS ARE, MASTER WINDU. LEAVE AT ONCE YOU WILL--

CHANCELLOR PALPATINE'S OFFICE FOR MASTER YODA.

CHANCELLOR PALPATINE, NEWS YOU HAVE?

NOT REGARDING THIS FORMIDABLE STARSHIP EVERYONE IS SO CONCERNED ABOUT, MASTER YODA...

...BUT I *WILL* REQUIRE THE SERVICES OF ANAKIN SKYWALKER FOR A MISSION OF IMPORTANCE TO THE REPUBLIC.

OF COURSE. AT YOUR DISPOSAL, HE IS.

THE CHANCELLOR YOU HEARD, SKYWALKER. AND MAY THE FORCE BE WITH YOU ALL.

YES, MASTER... BUT...

I'M SURE WE'LL FIND A REPLACEMENT FOR YOU, ANAKIN...

...AND I THINK I ALREADY KNOW *WHO*. AHSOKA, WE HAVE A *MISSION.*

YES, MASTER KENOBI. YOU, MASTER SKYWALKER, AND ME?

NOT QUITE, SNIPS...

...I WON'T BE WITH YOU ON THIS ONE. BUT I'M SURE YOU'LL DO FINE.

YES, MASTER, BUT...WHERE *WILL* YOU BE?

ANAKIN'S PLAYING *ERRAND BOY* FOR THE CHANCELLOR AGAIN. NICE TO BE TEACHER'S PET, *EH?*

JEALOUS? CHANCELLOR PALPATINE KNOWS THE *BEST* WHEN HE SEES IT, JYL.

STOP IT...!

A GOOD JEDI GOES WHERE THE FORCE *SENDS* HIM! *YOU'D* KNOW THAT, IF--!

WHOA, AHSOKA--SHE WAS JUST *KIDDING!* JYL AND I GO *WAY* BACK!

SINCE WE WERE JUST *YOUNGLINGS!* WE HAVE TO WORK TOGETHER. I HOPE WE CAN BE *FRIENDS,* SNIPS.

MY NAME IS *AHSOKA--* "MASTER" JYL.

25

CHANCELLOR PALPATINE, HOW MAY THE JEDI BE OF SERVICE?

AH, ANAKIN! YOU MAY BE OF SERVICE TO THE REPUBLIC...

...BY DELIVERING THESE SEEDS TO THE GOVERNMENT OF *DALTARRI.* AS PLANT-BASED BEINGS, THEY WILL SEE THIS AS A SIGN OF *GOODWILL.*

THAT'S *IT?* JUST DELIVER SOME *SEEDS?*

PATIENCE, ANAKIN! ONE NEVER KNOWS HOW LONG IT WILL TAKE A SEED TO *BEAR FRUIT!*

"...AND I THINK OUR PLAN WORKED! OUR ASSAULT SUMMONED THE *STARCRUSHER*...

"...THEY'RE DEPLOYING A SHUTTLE. *HMM,* I'M NOT READING ANY LIFE FORMS."

THIS MAY BE OUR ONLY CHANCE! YOU HAVE YOUR ORDERS!

YES, MASTER! OUR SHUTTLE HAS BEEN PROGRAMMED AS YOU DIRECTED!

CAPTAIN, YOU'VE DONE YOUR JOB. ORDER YOUR CRUISERS TO *DEPART!*

IT'S AGAINST OUR *NATURE* TO *FLEE*, MASTER WINDU -- BUT I UNDERSTAND! GOOD LUCK!

FUEL TANKER *AURORA* TO *STARCRUSHER*: IT SEEMS YOUR VERY *APPEARANCE* HAS BROKEN THE WILL OF THE REPUBLIC CRUISERS, ADMIRAL KIRST...!

...THERE WILL BE *NO NEED* FOR YOU TO --

CAPTAIN JORM --!

"--I READ A *SHUTTLE* PULLING AWAY FROM THE *AFT AIRLOCK,* SIR!"

WHAT--?

IT SEEMS YOU SPOKE *TOO SOON,* CAPTAIN! LET MY DROIDS BOARD YOUR LITTLE SHIP TO SWEEP FOR *INTRUDERS--*

--AND WE'LL TAKE CARE OF THAT TROUBLESOME *SHUTTLE,* TOO!

CROOM!

PLEASE CONVEY MY *BEST WISHES* TO ADMIRAL KIRST, AND...AND --

MY, *THEY* WERE CERTAINLY RUDE! PREPARE TO LEAVE THE SYSTEM!

THE DROIDS ARE RETURNING, ADMIRAL KIRST. THEIR DOWNLOAD READS NO REPORT WITH HOSTILES.

I *KNEW* IT! WHATEVER THE REPUBLIC WAS ATTEMPTING, IT *DIED* WITH THEIR SHUTTLE!

ALL RIGHT, YOU DROIDS, YOU HAVE YOUR ORDERS! STRAIGHT TO *MAINTENANCE*, AND THEN--

KRNNG!

OWWW--!

JUST IN *TIME!* I MIGHT NOT HAVE BEEN ABLE TO STAY HIDDEN THERE FOR MUCH LONGER!

AHSOKA--YOU, MASTER SOMTAY, AND I WILL SABOTAGE THE *LIFE-SUPPORT* SYSTEMS! OBI-WAN AND KI-ADI-MUNDI SHALL DISABLE THE *WEAPONS ARRAY!*

"...ABANDON SHIP!"

FWOOOOSH!

SURRENDER, AND THERE WILL BE NO--

WHAT--?

STAND DOWN! DROP ALL WEAPONS, OR--

MASTER *KI*..!

THIS IS CERTAINLY ODD.

...THERE IS NO *CREW.*

CURIOUS.

MASTER KI --

--THE SHIP SEEMS *DESERTED.* BUT HOW CAN THAT BE?

SOME *ESCAPE PODS* WERE LAUNCHED...BUT NOT NEARLY ENOUGH TO ACCOUNT FOR THE *ENTIRE CREW...*

"BACK TO THE *HANGAR BAY*-- IMMEDIATELY."

WHAT'S THIS *ABOUT,* MASTERS?

I FEEL A DISTURBANCE IN THE FORCE! THIS IS *NOT* RIGHT!

THE HANGAR BAY IS RIGHT AHEAD --

IS EVERYONE *ALL RIGHT?*

I BELIEVE *SO,* MASTER --

I FEAR WE HAVE BEEN *FOOLS,* MORE EASILY DECEIVED THAN THE MOST NAIVE *YOUNGLING...*

...THESE MECHANISMS ARE *HOLLOW* -- THEY ARE ONLY *SHELLS!*

LOOK AT *THIS,* MASTERS...

...THIS *CONSOLE* IS *EMPTY* -- JUST A *BOX* WITH SOME FLASHING LIGHTS. THEY *ALL* ARE.

AND SO --

40

ABANDONED, AS I THOUGHT.

BUT...WHAT DID THEY HOPE TO *GAIN?*

I THINK THEY WANTED US TO ACCOMPANY THIS FALSE SHIP ON ITS *FINAL JOURNEY* --

"-- INTO THIS SYSTEM'S *SUN.*"

THE SITUATION IS AS BAD AS WE *SUSPECTED.* THIS *"SHIP"* IS *HOLLOW,* WITH LITTLE *POWER* AND NO *NAVIGATIONAL CAPABILITY.*

THAT *LURCH* WE FELT WAS MOST OF ITS REMAINING POWER BEING EXPENDED AS IT SHIFTED *COURSE.*

EVEN THE *LIFE-SUPPORT* SYSTEM IS A FACSIMILE, *USELESS.*

WE HAVE AIR TO BREATHE, BUT WITHOUT THE OTHER SYSTEMS, EVENTUALLY THE SHIP WILL GROW *COLD.*

COLD, MASTER KI?

I DON'T THINK *COLD* WILL BE A PROBLEM!

YOU CAN CALL ME *"SNIPS."*

AND ON THE PLANET *DALTARRI*...

"THANK YOU FOR YOUR *OUTREACH,* MASTER SKYWALKER --"

--YOU MAY CONVEY TO CHANCELLOR PALPATINE OUR BEST WISHES IN YOUR STRUGGLE AGAINST THE SEPARATISTS...

...AND THANK HIM FOR HIS *GIFT*-- THE SEEDS WHOSE STRENGTHS WE WILL BLEND WITH OUR *OWN.*

THANK YOU, SIR...MADAM...*ER*... YOUR GRACE...

TELL THE CHANCELLOR THAT WE DALTARRI VALUE ABOVE ALL ELSE OUR **ALLIES**... THOSE WHO WILL AID YOU WITHOUT **QUESTION**.

WE, TOO, APPRECIATE OUR ALLIES, AND --

PLEASE **PARDON** ME, YOUR GRACE --

-- I HATE TO CUT OUR VISIT **SHORT**, BUT I MUST **DEPART**... ON URGENT BUSINESS.

UNDERSTOOD, MASTER SKYWALKER. MAY YOU HAVE SUNLIGHT, ABUNDANT WATER, AND DEEP **ROOTS**.

FIRE UP THE **ENGINES**, ARTOO-DETOO -- WE'RE **LEAVING**.

VADA BLOOT? WHEET?

47

...BUT RIGHT NOW, WE HAVE A *MORE IMPORTANT* MISSION!

TWOOOT

HOLD IT A SECOND. THERE'S SOMETHING --

I FEEL IT, TOO. MAYBE WE HAVE A *STOW-AWAY?*

I DON'T --

?!

WOW! THAT'S AN *AFFIRMATIVE!*

BDOW!

49

IF YOU'RE IN A HUGE HULK OF A STARSHIP THAT'S DRIFTING TOWARD THIS SYSTEM'S *SUN*--

-- I THINK I'M RIGHT *OUTSIDE!*

I'VE DEFIED THE CHANCELLOR'S *ORDERS.* IT'S THAT *REBELLIOUS STREAK* OF MINE YOU KEEP CAUTIONING ME ABOUT, I'M AFRAID!

BLESS THAT REBELLIOUS STREAK! FOR ONCE, YOU'RE RIGHT WHERE I *WANT* YOU!

WE'RE ON THE *BRIDGE,* ANAKIN. WE CAN *SEE* YOU! HERE'S WHAT WE NEED YOU TO *DO* --

UH-OH...!

VA-DA BLOOT?

YOU'RE *RIGHT,* ARTOO --THIS *IS* A BIG SHIP!

NOW WHAT DO I DO, MASTER?

JUST KEEP DRAWING THEIR FIRE!

LIEUTENANT DAAN, GIVE ME THE COORDINATES FOR THE *STARCRUSHER'S ENGINE ROOM!*

I *CAN'T* DO THAT! UP TO NOW I WAS COOPERATING TO SAVE MY *LIFE* -- *THAT* WILL MAKE ME A *TRAITOR!*

THE INSTANT SKYWALKER STOPS *DISTRACTING* THEM, THEY'LL FIRE ON *US!* THEY'LL GLADLY *SACRIFICE* YOU TO DESTROY US!

ALL RIGHT--*ALL RIGHT!*

ANAKIN, I'M TRANSMITTING THE COORDINATES FOR THEIR *POWER GENERATOR*--!

GOT IT, MASTER!

DO YOU *MEAN* YOU HAVEN'T DESTROYED THAT SHIP YET?

ADD MORE *TROOPS!*

YES, SIR...!

THEY HAVEN'T STOPPED HIM YET, ADMIRAL.

SEND *EVERY* AVAILABLE DROID! HE MUST BE STOPPED BEFORE HE REACHES--

--THE POWER GENERATOR...

EMERGENCY LIGHTING!

MISSION ACCOMPLISHED, MASTER!

GOOD JOB, ANAKIN! NOW GET *OUT* OF THERE, AS QUICKLY AS POSSIBLE!

66

EVERYONE, *AWAY* FROM THE BUTTRESSES--*!*

--AND THE *HULL!*

CLIKT

THUNK!

YOU'VE *MAGNETIZED* THE HULL? FOR WHAT *PURPOSE?*

FOR A *SOLUTION--* IF THE *FORCE* IS WITH US...

"...AND IF ANAKIN HAS DONE HIS *JOB*."

WE HAVE *NO POWER?* NOT EVEN *THRUSTERS?*

NOTHING, ADMIRAL! EVEN *COMMUNICATIONS* ARE OUT! I RECOMMEND--

PROOOOM

WHAT WAS *THAT*--?

IT FELT LIKE A *COLLISION...*

...BUT WITH *WHAT?*

MASTER *KENOBI?* NOT TO QUESTION YOUR *WISDOM...*

...BUT NOW WE'RE BEING DRAWN TO THE SUN EVEN MORE *QUICKLY!* HOW IS THIS A *SOLUTION?*

THE PADAWAN'S QUESTION IS A *WISE* ONE, OBI-WAN!

PATIENCE, MY FELLOW JEDI. WE'VE CAST OUT THE *BAIT*...

"...NOW WE MUST SEE IF OUR QUARRY TAKES THE *HOOK.*"

ADMIRAL KIRST TO *ALL* PERSONNEL...

...REPORT TO YOUR ASSIGNED **ESCAPE PODS** IMMEDIATELY! THIS IS **NOT** A DRILL!

FWOOOOSHT

THERE THEY *GO...*

AND WE'RE *NEXT!*

WE HAVEN'T GIVEN UP *YET!*

GET READY...

LIEUTENANT DAAN, I HOPE YOU DISCONNECTED THE *MAGNETIC COIL* -- OR THIS WILL BE A VERY *SHORT* TRIP!

AS YOU *ORDERED,* MASTER KENOBI! BUT--

IS THAT *TETHER* GOOD AND TIGHT? THEN HERE WE *GO...*

THERE'S ANAKIN!

NOW, ARTOO!

KLATCH

TRY TO REMAIN CALM, MASTERS! I'VE CALLED FOR TRANSPORT. IT SHOULD BE HERE SOON!

NOT TOO FAST, ANAKIN...!

ABOUT *YOU...* MASTER!

WHAT I WOULDN'T GIVE TO BE A ZESS-FLY ON THE WALL FOR *THAT* CONVERSATION!

THE JEDI HAVE **WON** THIS TIME. THEY HAVE WON AGAIN.

BUT HIS PATIENCE IS AS INFINITE AS THE **FORCE.** HE HAS **OTHER** SCHEMES...

...HIS VICTORY WILL BE ALL THE *SWEETER* FOR ITS LONG DELAY.

THE END

PRESIDENT AND PUBLISHER **MIKE RICHARDSON**

EXECUTIVE VICE PRESIDENT **NEIL HANKERSON**

CHIEF FINANCIAL OFFICER **TOM WEDDLE**

VICE PRESIDENT OF PUBLISHING **RANDY STRADLEY**

VICE PRESIDENT OF BOOK TRADE SALES **MICHAEL MARTENS**

VICE PRESIDENT OF BUSINESS AFFAIRS **ANITA NELSON**

VICE PRESIDENT OF MARKETING **MICHA HERSHMAN**

VICE PRESIDENT OF PRODUCT DEVELOPMENT **DAVID SCROGGY**

VICE PRESIDENT OF INFORMATION TECHNOLOGY **DALE LAFOUNTAIN**

SENIOR DIRECTOR OF PRINT, DESIGN, AND PRODUCTION **DARLENE VOGEL**

GENERAL COUNSEL **KEN LIZZI**

EDITORIAL DIRECTOR **DAVEY ESTRADA**

SENIOR MANAGING EDITOR **SCOTT ALLIE**

SENIOR BOOKS EDITOR **CHRIS WARNER**

EXECUTIVE EDITOR **DIANA SCHUTZ**

DIRECTOR OF PRINT AND DEVELOPMENT **CARY GRAZZINI**

ART DIRECTOR **LIA RIBACCHI**

DIRECTOR OF SCHEDULING **CARA NIECE**

STAR WARS GRAPHIC NOVEL TIMELINE (IN YEARS)

Omnibus: Tales of the Jedi—5,000–3,986 BSW4
Knights of the Old Republic—3,964–3,963 BSW4
The Old Republic—3653, 3678 BSW4
Knight Errant—1,032 BSW4
Jedi vs. Sith—1,000 BSW4
Omnibus: Rise of the Sith—33 BSW4
Episode I: The Phantom Menace—32 BSW4
Omnibus: Emissaries and Assassins—32 BSW4
Twilight—31 BSW4
Omnibus: Menace Revealed—31–22 BSW4
Darkness—30 BSW4
The Stark Hyperspace War—30 BSW4
Rite of Passage—28 BSW4
Honor and Duty—22 BSW4
Blood Ties—22 BSW4
Episode II: Attack of the Clones—22 BSW4
Clone Wars—22–19 BSW4
Clone Wars Adventures—22–19 BSW4
General Grievous—22–19 BSW4
Episode III: Revenge of the Sith—19 BSW4
Dark Times—19 BSW4
Omnibus: Droids—5.5 BSW4
Boba Fett: Enemy of the Empire—3 BSW4
Underworld—1 BSW4
Episode IV: A New Hope—SW4
Classic Star Wars—0–3 ASW4
A Long Time Ago . . . —0–4 ASW4
Empire—0 ASW4
Rebellion—0 ASW4
Boba Fett: Man with a Mission—0 ASW4
Omnibus: Early Victories—0–3 ASW4
Jabba the Hutt: The Art of the Deal—1 ASW4
Episode V: The Empire Strikes Back—3 ASW4
Omnibus: Shadows of the Empire—3.5–4.5 ASW4
Episode VI: Return of the Jedi—4 ASW4
Omnibus: X-Wing Rogue Squadron—4–5 ASW4
Heir to the Empire—9 ASW4
Dark Force Rising—9 ASW4
The Last Command—9 ASW4
Dark Empire—10 ASW4
Boba Fett: Death, Lies, and Treachery—10 ASW4
Crimson Empire—11 ASW4
Jedi Academy: Leviathan—12 ASW4
Union—19 ASW4
Chewbacca—25 ASW4
Invasion—25 ASW4
Legacy—130–137 ASW4

Old Republic Era
25,000 – 1000 years before
Star Wars: A New Hope

Rise of the Empire Era
1000 – 0 years before
Star Wars: A New Hope

Rebellion Era
0 – 5 years after
Star Wars: A New Hope

New Republic Era
5 – 25 years after
Star Wars: A New Hope

New Jedi Order Era
25+ years after
Star Wars: A New Hope

Legacy Era
130+ years after
Star Wars: A New Hope

Vector
Crosses four eras in the timeline

Volume 1
Knights of the Old Republic Volume 5
Dark Times Volume 3
Volume 2
Rebellion Volume 4
Legacy Volume 6

BSW4 = before *Episode IV: A New Hope*. ASW4 = after *Episode IV: A New Hope*.

FOR MORE ADVENTURE IN A GALAXY FAR, FAR, AWAY...

**STAR WARS: THE CLONE WARS—
THE WIND RAIDERS OF TALORAAN**
978-1-59582-231-4 | $7.99

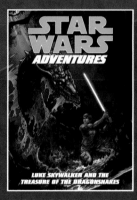

**STAR WARS ADVENTURES:
LUKE SKYWALKER AND THE
TREASURE OF THE DRAGONSNAKES**
978-1-59582-347-2 | $7.99

**STAR WARS ADVENTURES:
HAN SOLO AND THE
HOLLOW MOON OF KHORYA**
978-1-59582-198-0 | $7.99

**STAR WARS ADVENTURES:
PRINCESS LEIA AND THE ROYAL
RANSOM**
978-1-59582-147-8 | $7.99

**STAR WARS ADVENTURES:
THE WILL OF DARTH VADER**
978-1-59582-435-6 | $7.99

**STAR WARS: THE CLONE WARS—
THE COLOSSUS OF DESTINY**
978-1-59582-416-5 | $7.99

**STAR WARS: THE CLONE WARS—
SHIPYARDS OF DOOM**
978-1-59582-207-9 | $7.99

**STAR WARS: THE CLONE WARS—
CRASH COURSE**
978-1-59582-230-7 | $7.99

**STAR WARS: THE CLONE WARS—
SLAVES OF THE REPUBLIC**
978-1-59582-349-6 | $9.99

**STAR WARS: THE CLONE WARS—
IN SERVICE OF THE REPUBLIC**
978-1-59582-487-5 | $7.99

**STAR WARS: THE CLONE WARS—
HERO OF THE CONFEDERACY**
978-1-59582-552-0 | $7.99

**STAR WARS: THE CLONE WARS—
DEADLY HANDS OF SHON-JU**
978-1-59582-545-2 | $7.99

DARK HORSE BOOKS
darkhorse.com

AVAILABLE AT YOUR LOCAL COMICS SHOP OR BOOKSTORE

To find a comics shop in your area, call 1-888-266-4226
For more information or to order direct: • On the web: darkhorse.com • E-mail: mailorder@darkhorse.com
Phone: 1-800-862-0052 Mon.–Fri. 9 AM to 5 PM Pacific Time.
STAR WARS © 2004–2010 Lucasfilm Ltd. & ™ (BL8031)

STAR WARS
CLONE WARS ADVENTURES

Don't miss any of the action-packed adventures of your favorite **STAR WARS**® characters, available at comics shops and bookstores in a galaxy near you!

$6.99 each!